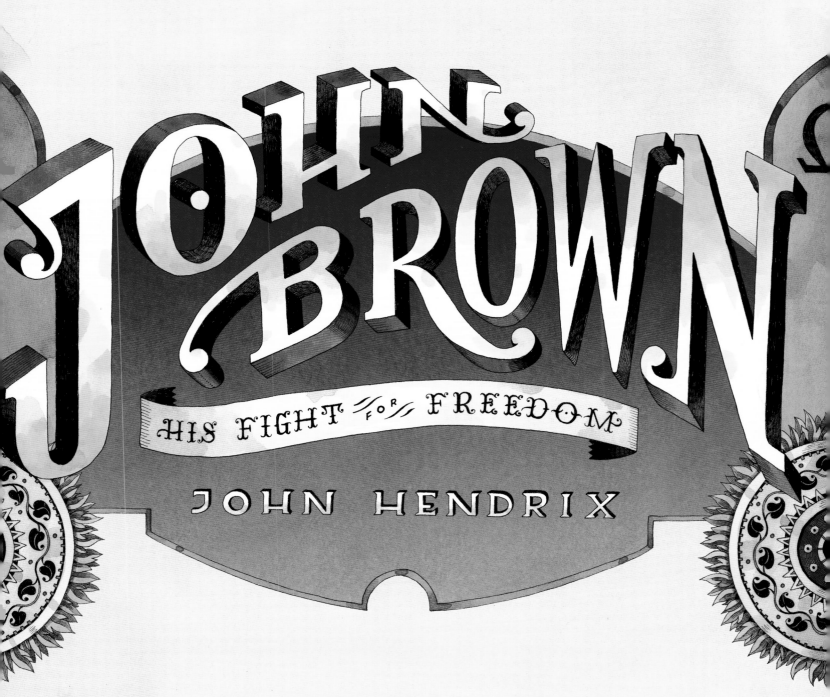

JOHN BROWN

HIS FIGHT FOR FREEDOM

JOHN HENDRIX

ABRAMS BOOKS FOR YOUNG READERS
NEW YORK

IN

1840 John Brown and his family lived in the small community of Hudson, in the state of Ohio. Hudson was a great center of the abolitionist cause. Abolitionists were people who believed that slavery was wrong and must end in the United States. Many whites in Hudson were opposed to slavery, but John felt even more strongly. He wanted black people to be treated as equal to white people. He and his family loved and respected their free black neighbors. They would often invite them over for dinner. They would sing together and stay up late telling stories. As a sign of respect, John always made sure to call them by their proper names, and not by their first names or nicknames like many white people would do.

GOOD MORNING

Ohio was called a "free state," because it didn't allow slavery. Before the Civil War, many states allowed white people to own black people and treat them like property. Millions of black men, women, and children were slaves without the hope of ever becoming free. The color of their skin became a badge of servitude and a license for others to despise them. But John knew that one man owning another was an abomination!

John's father, Owen, was also an abolitionist. He and John both ran stops on what came to be known as the Underground Railroad. This was a secret, connected line of safe houses where escaping slaves could stay as they made their way north to refuge in Canada. John would smuggle escaped slaves to the next stop using furniture wagons.

He was a devout Christian, also like his father. He taught his family to love God with all their hearts, and to love their neighbor just as much, even if that neighbor was different from them.

One Sunday at church, John and his family were escorted to the front pew, their usual seat. He turned to greet the preacher and saw that the entire back pew was filled with his black friends. John was not happy.

He stood and offered the entire black section his front pew. He escorted them to the best seats in the house, as his family went to sit in their seats in the back pew, behind the wood stove! At the end of the service, the white church members were very angry and demanded that John and his family leave the church immediately.

John Brown
was furious.

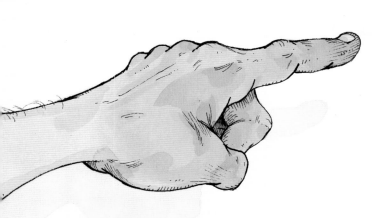

BEHOLD THE TEARS OF
SUCH AS WERE OPPRESSED
AND THEY HAD NO COMFORTER,
AND ON THE SIDE OF THEIR
OPPRESSORS THERE WAS POWER;
BUT THEY HAD NO COMFORTER.
· · ·
ECCLESIASTES 4:1

Upon reading these words, John felt a tremendous force growing inside his chest. He would never forget the day he discovered these words; it was then he made an oath to fight slavery until its very roots were destroyed. So John began to formulate a plan of grand liberation. This plan would not free one man at a time—it would free thousands.

"I WILL RAISE A STORM

IN THIS COUNTRY THAT WILL NOT BE STAYED SO LONG AS THERE IS A

SLAVE ON ITS SOIL."

By 1847 John's actions had gathered some attention in the black community. The former slave and famous abolitionist Frederick Douglass came to meet with him. John explained his plan to end slavery forever. He did not want a bloody war. His plan was based on economics. He would cause slavery to collapse by making the ownership of slaves vulnerable. The way he planned to do this was with liberation raids. Armed with specially made long spears, called pikes, John and his allies would free slaves in small groups and send them into the Allegheny Mountains. The weary would head north to Canada on the Underground Railroad, and the stronger would join John's freedom army. If owners could not rely on their slaves staying put as a constant workforce, then owners could

IS THE COST of LIBERTY

not be sure that they would have crops and other goods to sell. John hoped that slave merchants would have to raise prices to regain their lost profits, slowly making slavery too expensive for small farmers. If all went well, the rumors of the raids and possible rebellion would spread fears of economic ruin. More important, they would awaken the country to the horrors of slavery.

Frederick was greatly impressed with this mighty foe of slavery. No white man had ever suggested to him a willingness to literally fight and die for the cause of his race. Frederick admired John, but was unsure that his plan could work without great suffering.

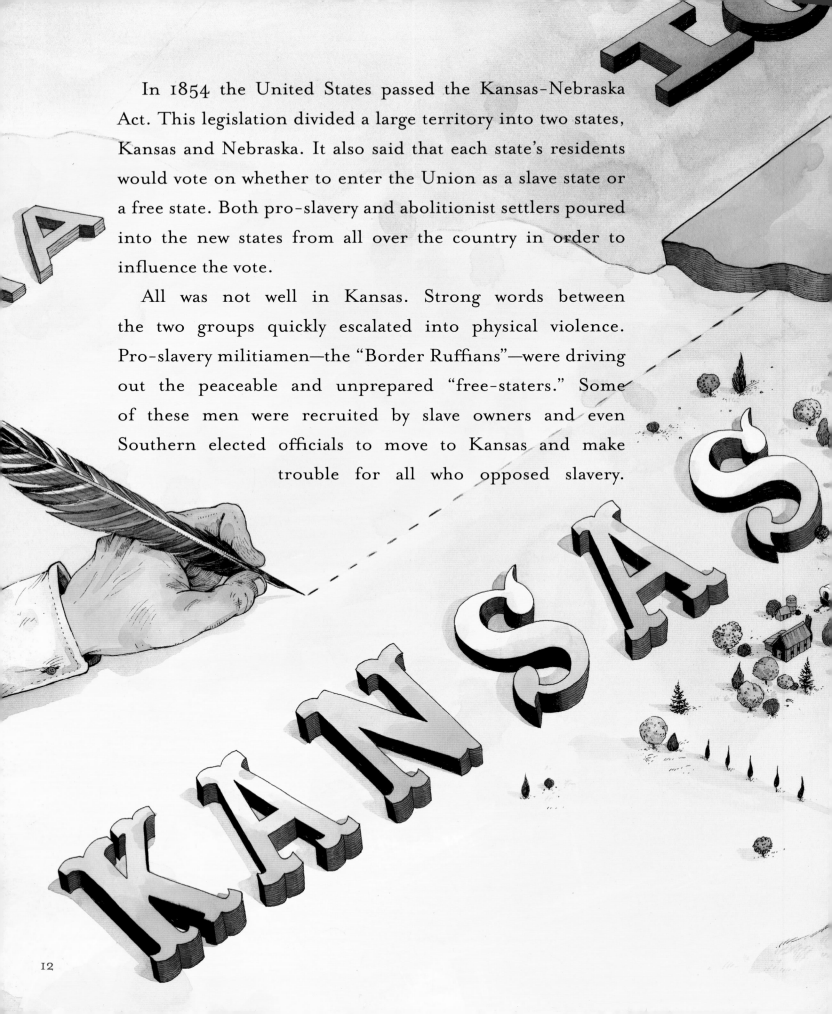

In 1854 the United States passed the Kansas-Nebraska Act. This legislation divided a large territory into two states, Kansas and Nebraska. It also said that each state's residents would vote on whether to enter the Union as a slave state or a free state. Both pro-slavery and abolitionist settlers poured into the new states from all over the country in order to influence the vote.

All was not well in Kansas. Strong words between the two groups quickly escalated into physical violence. Pro-slavery militiamen—the "Border Ruffians"—were driving out the peaceable and unprepared "free-staters." Some of these men were recruited by slave owners and even Southern elected officials to move to Kansas and make trouble for all who opposed slavery.

Determined to make Kansas a slave state at any cost, the Ruffians destroyed crops, burned entire settlements, and killed those who got in their way.

Like a great fuming tornado, John swept across the plains to fight for Kansas. He fought many battles on those windy plains, but it was a dark night along Pottawatomie Creek that made him notorious. John and his sons stormed the houses of five pro-slavery settlers who had been threatening his family and other abolitionists, took the men to the creek, and killed them with broadswords.

John's ruthless tactics spread fear into the hearts of the Border Ruffians and others, but also branded John a crazed madman. Captain John Brown, as he came to be known, was a folk hero to many free-staters and an outlaw to the federal government. It was a savage and brutal period in what came to be known as "Bleeding Kansas."

Now a wanted man, John could not go home. He grew a long beard to disguise himself and traveled to Iowa, Ohio, New York, and Massachusetts. Along the way, John recruited men, both black and white, who would follow him in his fight against slavery. During his trip to the black communities in Canada, John met his greatest ally. Her name was Harriet Tubman. Harriet was a black woman who had escaped slavery in her youth. Over many years, she traveled amid great danger, personally leading more than three hundred individuals to freedom. John stayed at her home in Chatham, Ontario, and quickly discovered that she was a born leader.

At dinner one evening, she heard John's long-planned dream of grand liberation. Her eyes gleamed, and she swore to fight by his side! From that time on, he took to calling her . . .

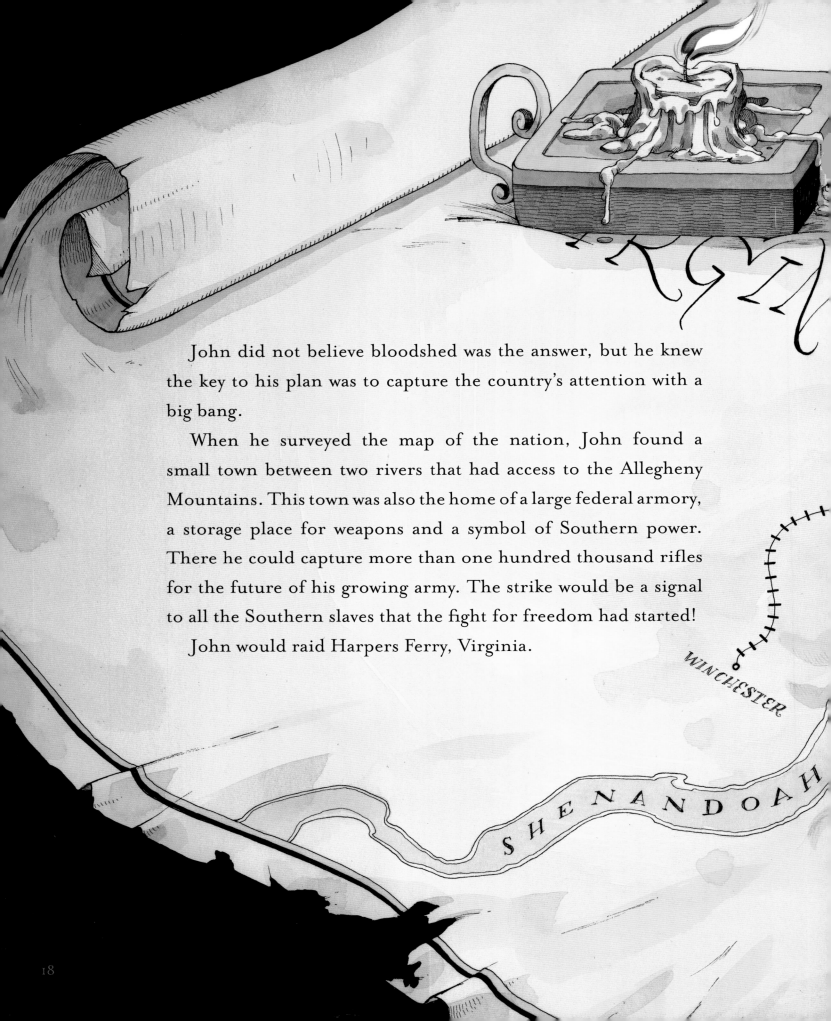

John did not believe bloodshed was the answer, but he knew the key to his plan was to capture the country's attention with a big bang.

When he surveyed the map of the nation, John found a small town between two rivers that had access to the Allegheny Mountains. This town was also the home of a large federal armory, a storage place for weapons and a symbol of Southern power. There he could capture more than one hundred thousand rifles for the future of his growing army. The strike would be a signal to all the Southern slaves that the fight for freedom had started!

John would raid Harpers Ferry, Virginia.

WINCHESTER

SHENANDOAH

SHEPHERDSTOWN

POTOMAC RIVER

MARYL

HARPERS FERRY

RIVER

FREDERICK

B&O RAILROAD

N

While he was planning the attack, Harriet Tubman was stricken ill—a devastating blow to John's plan. He knew that he needed a black leader by his side to help him win the respect and trust of the slaves he was liberating. Without a black voice of authority, John feared that his army of ex-slaves would not follow him. There was only one person John could ask for help.

John met secretly with Frederick Douglass to plead with him to join his force. Frederick deeply respected John and believed

in him, but he did not believe in his plan. Frederick was confident that such an attack on a federal building would turn the country against them and the only result would be martyrdom. John could not convince him otherwise. But it was too late to change the plan. The raid would have to continue without Frederick's support.

John secretly contacted the twenty-one men he had assembled to help with the raid. He gave them instructions to meet at the farmhouse of R. F. Kennedy just outside of Harpers Ferry.

In the early dark hours of Monday, October 17, 1859, it all began.

John led the assault on the armory. Swiftly coming down the mountain to the riverside, he and his men cut telegraph wires, took the bridge, and crossed the Potomac River into Harpers Ferry. The armory was guarded by only one watchman and was easily secured as the town slept. The operation was going as planned. John's raiders also took several hostages from around the town, including Colonel Lewis Washington, the great-grandnephew of George Washington.

But later that morning, things started to go wrong. A train full of passengers heading to Baltimore, Maryland, pulled into Harpers Ferry. Unwilling to take so many hostages, John allowed the train to continue.

But before the train left, something horrible happened. The baggage master came searching for the missing armory watchman and was shot dead by one of the raiders. The first man killed during the raid was a free black man, Shephard Hayward.

The unfolding events shook John to the core. He became a hesitant leader. Time was passing, and so was the opportunity to escape. Townsmen had taken notice of the attack. Shots were ringing out from local farmers who had taken positions on the high ground above the armory. By noon they were joined by a number of well-organized militia companies from neighboring towns.

John's men and their hostages were driven inside the small brick engine house next to the armory. Several of his raiders had been killed by rifle fire, and others were pinned down in the armory while retreating from the bridge. Three raiders were still waiting at a schoolhouse across the Potomac to rendezvous with the fleeing raiders and escaped slaves. But the militia now held all the escape routes from the town, leaving John and his men cornered in the engine house. John saw it was too late. Escape across the bridge would cost many lives.

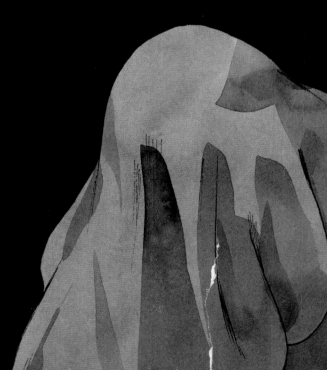

John hadn't thought he'd be in Harpers Ferry long enough to regret letting that train go, but it proved to be a huge mistake. The train swiftly carried word of the raid straight to Washington. As the capital buzzed with news later that morning, the U.S. Marines were dispatched to retake the town. That night, a large force of soldiers marched into Harpers Ferry led by Robert E. Lee and J. E. B. Stewart, future leaders of the Confederate Army.

By dawn on Tuesday, the Marines had John and his men surrounded and demanded an unconditional surrender. When John refused, Colonel Lee ordered his men to storm the engine house. The raiders fought back but were hopelessly outnumbered.

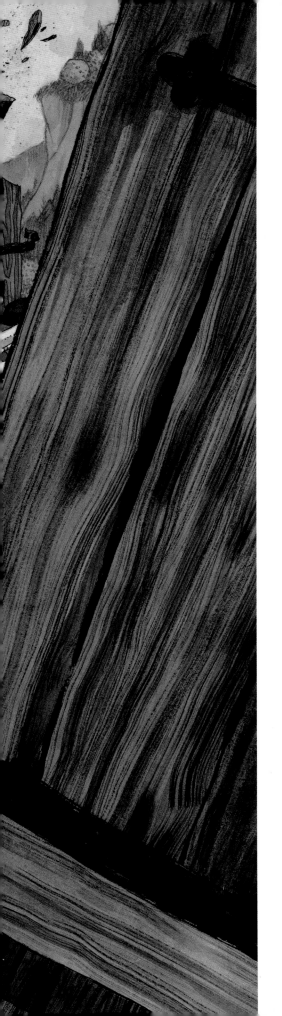

Those who were there that day said something amazing happened during that siege. Lieutenant Israel Green, who led the assault, spotted John and drew his sword to cut him down. His mighty lunge hit John's belt, and his sword bent in half! The marine had accidentally carried his lightweight dress sword, and not his heavy combat sword. John was severely injured but was captured alive.

John's war against slavery had ended.

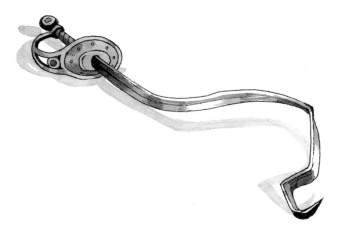

Sparing no time for him to recover, the soldiers immediately took John to Charlestown, Virginia, and put him on trial for insurrection, conspiracy, and high treason. He was so badly injured that he rested on a cot throughout the proceedings.

John's lawyers begged him to plead insanity in order to persuade the judge to spare his life. But John refused to accept this defense because it would damage the cause of abolition in the eyes of the world. At the end of a rushed trial, John was able to rise to his feet for the verdict. He was sentenced to death!

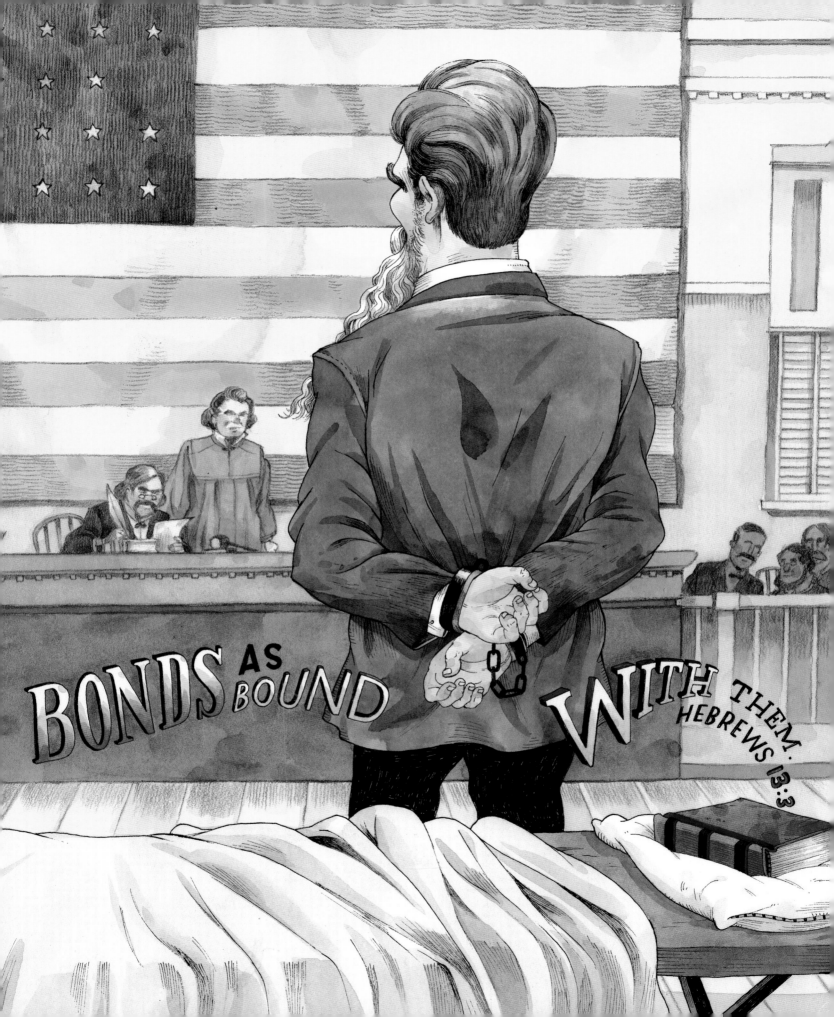

On December 2, 1859, the wagon arrived at John's jail cell to take him to the gallows. As John took his last look at this world, he was no longer angry.

"I DID NOT WRONG, BUT *RIGHT*. NOW, IF IT IS DEEMED NECESSARY THAT I SHOULD FORFEIT MY LIFE FOR THE FURTHERANCE OF THE ENDS OF *JUSTICE*, AND MINGLE MY BLOOD FURTHER WITH THE BLOOD OF MY CHILDREN AND WITH THE *BLOOD* OF MILLIONS IN THIS SLAVE COUNTRY WHOSE RIGHTS ARE DISREGARDED BY WICKED, CRUEL, AND UNJUST ENACTMENTS . . . SO **LET IT BE DONE.**"

John was buried on December 8, 1859, in the earth of those northern mountains that he hoped would guide thousands to freedom. Free blacks from all over the land came to attend the funeral.

John never lived to see a United States free of slavery. But in death, he accomplished what he could not in life. For the forty-five days between his capture and his death, John wrote many letters that were published in newspapers all around the country. The publicity surrounding his execution strengthened the abolitionist cause and rallied thousands to call for an end to slavery. Many people called him a crazy zealot and thought his scheme was a bloodthirsty act of terrorism. But others said he was a hero.

John Brown, the man who hated slavery, had proudly declared war upon that horrible practice. His war did not bring freedom, but his voice roused a complacent nation to action.

JOHN BROWN has been a

source of controversy for more than 150 years. In difficult times, men were forced to make difficult choices. When faced with the horrors of slavery, John could not bear the thought of inaction. This book is my interpretation of how a man who saw violent oppression chose to fight it, no matter the consequence. His decision to wage war on slavery in America made him an outlaw and ultimately cost him his life. But I think that his role in American history is often misunderstood.

Today it is hard to grasp the immense sense of desperation felt by John and people like him during the time in Kansas still referred to as "Bleeding Kansas." On those barren plains there were no laws, no protection for families, and no hope for justice. While reading about those events, I often asked myself, if I saw my neighbors threatened, my family terrorized, and my dearest friends hauled away in chains, what would I do? Would I strike back against injustice?

As I continued to study the life of John Brown, I began to admire him because he would not make a truce with injustice. Now, no man is perfect, and John was no exception. His ambitious plan to free the slaves was a spectacular failure. But though the United States hanged him as a traitor, I feel we must not dismiss him as a madman. Terrorists crave destruction and turmoil, and the seed of John's rebellion was compassion. Scholar Louis A. DeCaro Jr. writes of John Brown's concern for his hostages at Harpers Ferry:

"Few if any have criticized John Brown for his reckless compassion, or attributed his failure at Harpers Ferry to a worried devotion to the Golden Rule. Yet it was neither inept planning nor a lack of strategic support that proved his downfall at Harpers Ferry, but rather the same deep-rooted sympathy that had always driven him to the side of the downcast. Thinking that he could somehow balance the enemies' peace with the success of the mission, he was caught in a trap of his own making, but not the 'perfect steel trap' that Frederick Douglass predicted two months before. John Brown had done his homework well and easily captured the defenseless town and armory, and could just as easily have walked away had he not delayed. It was his own heartfelt blunder that allowed him to fall into the hands of the Old Dominion."

John was a devout believer in Christianity. He used the Bible's words—that men are loved and valuable to God—as a holy plumb line. When he held this truth up against the crooked world, he knew things should be different. I was astonished to read about John's belief that black people should not just be *free* but *equal*, which was an idea far outside mainstream abolitionism in the antebellum United States. His passion for freedom was undisputed. Frederick Douglass said of John Brown: "His zeal in the cause of my race was greater than mine. I could live for the slave, but he could die for him."

We should remember John Brown because he was not afraid to fight for the freedom of an oppressed people to which he did not belong. John was not a vigilante. The goals of his crusade were never mayhem, self-glorification, or personal vendetta, but freedom for all who were persecuted. It is difficult to say if his war against slavery was simply "right" or "wrong." Ultimately, John Brown's contribution was not freedom itself, but an unbridled vision of conviction.

IN THE TELLING OF THIS STORY, some events, conversations, and compositional staging have been reimagined to make them more appealing. But John Brown's personal state of mind, thoughts, and reflections are not imaginative speculation. They are collected from the hard work of other scholars, many of whom are listed in the bibliography. These scholars make their conclusions by combing through hundreds of letters and personal accounts of John's life. Of course, there can be many different verdicts drawn from the record of history, but I would encourage readers to study the life of John Brown and decide for themselves. If any facts have been left unsaid, it is only for the sake of brevity, and not a desire to present a tailored account of his life. For example, John Brown had twenty children—of whom only ten survived to adulthood—by two wives. To accurately recount the constant family changes to a casual reader would distract from the narrative. Also, the description of John's time in Kansas has been edited for length, not content. Indeed, entire books have been dedicated to John's time in "Bleeding Kansas," and it is well worth further exploration. And lastly, it is worth clarifying that while Harpers Ferry was part of Virginia at the time of John's raid, it was included as part of West Virginia when that state was founded in 1863.

SELECT SOURCES

In the numbers below in parentheses, the number before the colon indicates the page in this book where a direct quotation is used, and the number following the colon indicates the page in the source book where that quotation can be found. All biblical passages reproduced in this book are from the Authorized or King James Version of the Bible, in an edition published by the American Bible Society, New York, NY, 1854.

Carton, Evan. *Patriotic Treason: John Brown and the Soul of America.* New York, NY: Free Press, 2006.

Cohen, Stan. *John Brown: Thundering Voice of Jehovah; A Pictorial Heritage.* Missoula, MT: Pictorial Histories Publishing Co., Inc., 1999.

DeCaro Jr., Louis A. *Fire from the Midst of You: A Religious Life of John Brown.* New York, NY: New York University Press, 2002. (Pages 9:237)

——*John Brown: The Cost of Freedom; Selections from His Life and Letters.* New York, NY: International Publishers. 2007. (Pages 38:92)

Drake, Ross. "The Law That Ripped America in Two: 150 Years Ago the Kansas-Nebraska Act Set the Stage for Civil War." *Smithsonian,* May 2004.

Du Bois, W. E. B. *John Brown.* Philadelphia, PA: G. W. Jacobs, 1909. (Pages 10–11:230; 35:216)

Gopnik, Adam. "John Brown's Body." *New Yorker,* April 25, 2005.

Holland, Jesse J. *Black Men Built the Capitol.* Guilford, CT: Global Pequot Press, 2007. (Pages 39:115)

Oates, Stephen B. *To Purge This Land with Blood: A Biography of John Brown.* New York, NY: Oxford University Press, 1974.

Peterson, Merrill D. *John Brown, The Legend Revisited.* Charlottesville, VA: University of Virginia Press, 2002.

Reynolds, David S. *John Brown, Abolitionist: The Man Who Killed Slavery, Sparked Civil War, and Seeded Civil Rights.* New York, NY: Alfred A. Knopf, 2005.

INDEX

To Andrea, Jack, and Anneli, my first love.
To my parents, my sure foothold.
—J. H.

The illustrations in this book were made with pen and ink with fluid acrylic washes on Strathmore Vellum Bristol.

Library of Congress Cataloging-in-Publication Data
Hendrix, John, 1976–
John Brown / written and illustrated by John Hendrix.
p. cm.
ISBN 978-0-8109-3798-7 (Harry N. Abrams, Inc.)
1. Brown, John, 1800–1859–Juvenile literature. 2. Abolitionists—United States—Biography—Juvenile literature.
3. Antislavery movements—United States—History—19th century—Juvenile literature. I. Title.

E451.H46 2009
973.7'116092—dc22
[B]
2008045969

HNA ▌▌▌▌▌
harry n. abrams, inc.
a subsidiary of La Martinière Groupe
115 West 18th Street
New York, NY 10011
www.hnabooks.com